A TRANSCREATION
OF THE FOURTEENTH-CENTURY
MIDDLE ENGLISH POEM

Pearl

A TRANSCREATION
OF THE FOURTEENTH-CENTURY
MIDDLE ENGLISH POEM

J. D. Winter

sussex
ACADEMIC
PRESS
Brighton • Chicago • Toronto

2 4 6 8 10 9 7 5 3 1

First published 2019, in Great Britain by
SUSSEX ACADEMIC PRESS
PO Box 139
Eastbourne BN24 9BP

Distributed in North America by
SUSSEX ACADEMIC PRESS
Independent Publishers Group
814 N. Franklin Street, Chicago, IL 60610

British Library Cataloguing in Publication Data
A CIP catalogue record for this book is available from the British Library.

Library of Congress Cataloging-in-Publication Data
Names: Winter, Joe, 1943– translator.
Title: Pearl : a transcreation of the fourteenth-century Middle English poem / J.D. Winter.
Other titles: Pearl (Middle English poem). English (Winter)
Description: Brighton ; Chicago : Sussex Academic Press, [2019]
Identifiers: LCCN 2019013497 | ISBN 9781789760224 (paperback : alk. paper)
Subjects: LCSH: Pearl (Middle English poem)
Classification: LCC PR2111 .A21 2019 | DDC 821/.1—dc23
LC record available at https://lccn.loc.gov/2019013497

Typeset & designed by Sussex Academic Press, Brighton & Eastbourne.
Printed by TJ International, Padstow, Cornwall.

Contents

Introduction   1

PEARL   7
A transcreation of the 14th-century Middle English poem

Introduction

For about five hundred years *Pearl* appears to have lain bound up together with its remarkable cousin-poem *Gawain and the Green Knight* and two lesser poems in one private collection or another. They were written out in a late fourteenth-century hand and can safely be said to date from that period. Their common authorship, suggested by language use, is called into question by the perceived differences of tone and poetic type between *Pearl* and *Gawain*: a moot point and not a vital one set beside the fact of their existence. When one considers these two great poems and their loss to the world for half a millennium, one wonders what further marvels may have vanished from the comparatively tiny literary élites of the English tongue of the time, amongst whom in other regions were Chaucer and Langland. The spread of literacy, so marked since then, does not appear to carry the sense of poetry so noticeably in its wake. It may be that poetry attaches itself to a culture rich in oral tradition and commemorates that exactly: the speaking voice. On the page it may almost be defined as a voice speaking from paper. The quarto pages of vellum that are the record of the narrator's voice from the North-West Midlands so long ago speak in the clearest tones of the truest fact, that which has yielded to the alchemy of the imagination. It may be observed that the poem does not let go of a central mystery: the pearl's identity, though made apparent, is never quite surrendered to literal fact. The real world is not much to do with literal facts.

Literary scholars can sometimes have more to do with them and there has tended to be a curious focus of attention in the editorial and critical discussion the poem has so far received.

Certainly the theological debate is of some historical importance and the poet had a point to make. But the weight of the poem is to do with an internal struggle to be resolved at length in terms of personal diminution and increase. It is a journey of understanding, brilliantly lit, or of going beyond the self, that invites reflection on a vital aspect of the human experience. Or to put it differently, there is a change in the light the poem seeks to mirror. Perhaps, however, these things are best left for individual readers of the poem to mull over on their own and the scholars are right. In any case the attractions of *Gawain* (a courtly epic not deeply challenging on the personal level) have tended to draw the scholar's eye; and *Pearl* still has a pristine freshness in the great English canon. It was edited first in 1864 by Richard Morris and best in 1953 by E.V. Gordon. It has suffered a few translations into modern English but as yet the poetry has stayed in the original. My version preserves the overall flow and the shape of the original, the intricate stanza-form and locking keyword system (concatenation); but is light on the alliteration, that supplies both a dancing decoration and the sense of a driven need. What follows then is no more than a pale reflection, yet I hope a true one, and not without a poetic echo of its own.

The poetic conventions of alliteration (old) and rhyme (new) meet at a peak in *Pearl*; uniquely so in extant literature. The alliterated half-lines of Anglo-Saxon poetry are reborn in a powerful four-stress line in an elaborate stanza. Technically the poem is in a class of its own. The constant glittering effect does not stand apart from the theme, shining for its own sake, but enhances the richness of the "pearl" and what is around it, including finally the narrator's world. That such a demanding form is used with no sacrifice to superficiality, the poetry not once lapsing into the mere ornateness of verse, is a measure at deepest level of the validity of the exercise of writing. If a poem is a circle of truth, the description of a complete experience, the end justifying the initial adventure, *Pearl* is a circle as deeply-etched as any.

Many vision-poems were written then; *Piers Plowman* is probably the best-known. *Pearl* is compelling as a dream-rendering, perhaps above all in a suggestion of richness and transience in which clarity, detail and psychological accuracy all play a part. It is a threnody of loss and a poem of love, an explicitly Christian document carrying the truth (surely that of all religions) of eternal gain through the surrender of self-will. This is not lightly achieved: for above all *Pearl* is an authentic tale of conversion. It deals in human shortcomings and the ideal, the ground of their relation, in some evolution of the human. It deserves a better translation than it has found here, and should be read widely in the original. It is the most beautiful Christian poem.

JDW 2019

Pearl

Pearl

I

Pearl, fit for a prince's pleasure,
Flawless fellow to flashing gold,
In truth I declare, so dear a treasure
Even in the East's not bought or sold.
Though I examined all jewels at leisure,   5
Her every appearance seemed so bold,
I'd class her unique, out of all measure . . .
So round, small-sided, and smooth of mould.
Alas! away from me it rolled,
Through grass into a garden-plot.   10
I repine, hurt in love's powerful hold,
For that special pearl that had no spot.

Since in that spot it slipped from me
I have often looked and longed for that charm
That once removed all misery –   15
A source of great content and calm.
My heart is punished oppressively,
In sorrow my breast swells up, too warm;
Yet the sweetest sound it seems there could be
I heard in silence without alarm.   20
It brings many songs, that there is no balm
For her complexion, so covered in clot.
O earth, a pretty prize you harm,
My special pearl that had no spot.

That spot must be with spices spread   25
Where such a splendour suffers blight;
Blooms of yellow and blue and red
That sparkle sharply in sunlight.
Where it sank in soil the colour of lead
Flower and fruit are no less bright;   30
For each grass grows from grain that is dead;
No crops would be cut unless this were right.
From good each good will gather its might;
A seed of such virtue prevents it not
That spices press out, springing upright   35
From that precious pearl that had no spot.

To the spot of which in speech I tell
I ventured, into the garden green
In August, as the festival fell
When corn is cut with sickles keen.   40
Where the pearl was lost plants prospered well,
Shading the mound they sparkled clean,
Ginger, gillyflower and gromwell,
Peonies powdered in between.
If it was pretty, a sight to be seen,   45
The smell was surpassed by not a jot.
Look there, I thought, there lies a queen,
My precious pearl that had no spot.

Before that spot my hand I clenched;
An ice-cold care touched me and caught;   50
A hidden hurt at my heart wrenched,
Though reason left me less distraught.
I mourned my pearl there deep entrenched
With stubborn claims that closely fought;
With sorrow my wretched will was drenched;   55
Though Christ's own nature comfort taught.
I fell upon that flowery court,
So strong a smell to my brains shot;
And swiftly met with sleep's onslaught –
On that precious pearl that had no spot.   60

II

From that spot my spirit sprang up in a while;
My body lay dreaming on the mound.
My soul has spurred forth in God's smile,
Off on a quest where marvels abound.
I knew I was by a high rocky pile,   65
Yet knew not where on earth it was found;
Towards a forest I made trial
Where cliffs could be seen, fit to astound.
Their light must hold each one spell-bound,
The glory that gleamed from them, glinted away.   70
There's no fine fabric woven and wound
Of half so splendid a display.

Displayed were all those sloping sides
With crystal cliffs of sparkling stone.
Bright woods perch on them besides,   75
Trunks with blue of Indian;
Like polished silver each leaf slides,
To brim each branch with glancing tone;
When clear sky-gleam at them glides,
Shivering sharp and shrill they have shone.   80
Gravel that crunched as I trod on
Was precious pearls, all down the way.
Sunbeams are but dark and wan
In respect of that display.

Those slopes so sparkling in display   85
Rid my spirit of wretchedness.
The fragrant fruit-smells freshly stray,
Nourishing me like food, no less.
Birds are on their woodland way,
Flying together in flaming dress,   90
All sizes – and let all citoles play,
The lovely notes they'll not express.
As their wings the wood-air press
Birds' songs blend in harmony.
Nothing might a man more bless   95
Than that display to hear and see.

And so displayed quite splendidly
Was that fine wood where I was sent
By fate. To show such finery
No man the right verse might invent.   100
I walked right on, I felt so free;
No rise my progress could prevent;
Meadow and spice-plant and pear-tree,
The wood gave great astonishment,
Shrubs, hedgerows, banks – as on it went.   105
Like sharp thread-gold the sheer banks lay.
And then a stream before me bent.
Lord, brilliant was that display!

Displayed where it ran richly deep
Were beryl banks of marvellous flare.   110
The water swirled in its soft sweep,
Carrying its whispering course on there.
At the bottom stones their brightness keep,
As glass a gleaming ray will spare,
As a stream of stars, when earth-men sleep,   115
Let go their light through cold night-air.
And all were pebbles beyond compare,
Emeralds, sapphires, jewels that are gay,
Making the water shine rich and rare . . .
Of such delight was its display.   120

III

That grand display of hill and dale,
Of wood and water and splendid plain,
Charged me with joy – and broke the jail
Of grief, and put down all my pain.
Down by the stream and its strong trail   125
In bliss I turned with teeming brain.
I went along that watery vale,
My heart lay in joy's lovely strain:
As fortune acts with might and main
When sending either sweet or sore,   130
Whoever has the loss or gain
Will find he meets it more and more.

More wonders were there of that sort
Than I could tell though I had all day.
Earthly feelings fall far short   135
Regarding all that royal array;
And it was Paradise, I thought,
That over past the broad banks lay.
The stream could seem to run for sport,
Gardens grand all down its way;   140
And I thought too, not far away
Was a walled city over the shore.
But the water was deep, I had to stay –
Though longing always more and more.

More and more, and yet more too   145
I yearned to see beyond the brook.
If where I walked was fair, I knew
The far land had a lovelier look.
And so I stopped, to closely view
All round: and quickly undertook   150
To find some bridge. But the danger grew
As on my venturing steps I took.
Yet I kept thinking one should brook
A peril, with such joys in store . . .
And then a new thing came, that shook   155
My wondering mind still more and more.

More of a marvel dumbfounded me.
I saw now, past that pleasant stream,
A crystal cliff that dazzlingly
Shone: it shot out many a beam.   160
And at its foot sat, I could see,
A child, whose bearing made her seem
A girl of grace and courtesy,
Her mantle glittering a white gleam.
And she shone like a cut in a gold seam.   165
I knew her well, I had seen her before –
My eyes pursuing their new theme,
I found I knew her more and more.

The more I studied her fair face,
And her fine form had looked upon,   170
Such ecstasy gave me its grace
As I had rarely undergone.
And so my heart began to race
To call her – but my wits were gone;
I saw her in so strange a place,   175
My sense was shattered, not at one.
Her face she lifted: I looked on:
Ivory white the hue it wore.
Feelings and thoughts then had I none
Except amazement, more and more.   180

IV

More than I wished then, fear arose.
I stood dead still and dared not call.
Eyes wide, a mouth that would not unclose,
I stood as quiet as a hawk in a hall.
Heavenly truth could here disclose: 185
But yet I feared what might befall,
That she should escape whom my eyes chose,
Before I had talked with her at all.
That lovely maiden, lissom, small,
So fine, most gifted of all girls,   190
In royal dress now rose up tall,
A precious person set with pearls.

Pearls set out in princely show
It was my fortune then to see,
As down the bank began to go   195
That form. She was fresh as a fleur-de-lys.
Her linen garment shed a white glow,
Open at the sides and beautifully
Framed with the finest pearls, I know,
That had ever made their way near me.   200
With jewels (I know this certainly)
In double rows each wide sleeve swirls.
Her bright gown kept the harmony,
All set about with precious pearls.

A crown set out with jewels entire   205
She wore – it was of jewels alone.
Clear white pearls sprang up each spire,
Flowers were figured in the stone.
It was her only head-attire,
Her hair lay loose and on its own;   210
Her grave look one could well admire;
Her hue was whiter than whale's bone.
Like bright shorn gold her locks then shone,
Lying down her shoulders in long curls.
That wealth of colour lay well on   215
Embroidery set with precious pearls.

And she was set at every hem –
Wrist-bands, sides, neck-opening –
With white pearls and no other gem;
Clothes, too, were white-glittering.   220
But a marvellous pearl in the midst of them
Her breast-coat carried like a king.
Man's measurement it must condemn,
For it defied all reckoning –
A pearl past all imagining.   225
All words must sound the speech of churls
About so bright, clear, pure a thing
Set there, most precious among pearls.

That precious person, with pearls set,
Came down the bank and stood close by   230
The stream. From here to Greece you've met,
I'll vow, none happier than I.
No niece she is, but nearer yet;
And so my heart is lifted high.
She took off her rich coronet,   235
Bowed womanly low – to signify
She'd speak – then hailed me with a warm cry.
Such utter joy through my head whirls,
I bless my birth as I reply
To that sweet girl there, set with pearls!   240

V

'O pearl, set out with pearls,' said I,
'Are you the pearl of my lament,
Grieved for, as at night I lie?
So much sorrow has been spent
Since into grass you once slipped by.   245
Abject, broken, my heart is rent –
And you live lightly, never sigh,
In Paradise, in sweet assent.
What fate my jewel to this place sent,
And dealt me this despair, this danger?   250
Since we were parted and you went,
I have been a joyless jeweller.'

That jewel then, in her gems so fair,
Looked up – gray-eyed – set on her crown
So fine, and with a serious air   255
Said, 'Sir, your story's upside-down.
From its fine setting, you declare,
Your pearl is gone – and sigh and frown.
But sir, this royal garden's where
It is to its advantage shown: 260
Set here, where rancour is unknown –
So in delight to exist for ever.
O sir, this casket were your own,
If you were a generous jeweller.

'But gracious jeweller, if you lose   265
All joy for a gem that once in chief
You valued – a strange way you choose,
And act upon a false belief.
A rose it was, that nature imbues
But for a time with flower and leaf;   270
Now by a different nature's use
A pearl it proves, set in relief.
And you have called your fate a thief
That something out of nothing clear
Has given you. What cures your grief   275
You blame – an unjust jeweller.'

A jewel, in my opinion
Was she – as jewels her words excel.
'Indeed, my dear delightful one,
All my distress you quite dispel.   280
But I believed my pearl was gone –
And that was why my spirits fell.
But now I've found it: whereupon
In a bright wood with it I'll dwell;
And praise my Lord, his laws as well,   285
For to this bliss he brought me near.
To cross now, where these waters swell,
I'd be a joyful jeweller.'

'Jeweller,' said that gem so clear,
'You're jesting now – it's quite absurd! 290
You've said three things together here:
In each of them you've plainly erred.
And what they mean you've no idea –
Your wits are out on every word.
First, you tell yourself I'm near 295
Because you see my form, unblurred;
The second statement that I heard
Was that we'd live right here together.
You'd cross the stream, that was the third –
Which may no joyful jeweller. 300

VI

'That jeweller I little praise
Who in belief will go by eye,
And blind and churlish in his ways
Holds it that our Lord would lie.
Your life he promised to upraise 305
Though flesh in fortune's way must die;
But when the proof of all things stays
On sight – you set his words awry.
And it will scarcely dignify
A good man, to depend on pride, 310
When all report he would deny
Except what his own wits decide.

'Decide for yourself if your disjointed
Words are as a prayer should be.
Here your home you have appointed –   315
Not with leave, it seems to me.
And yet you might be disappointed.
To ford here, you must differently
Oppose yourself – be otherwise pointed –
Your flesh in earth lie frozenly.   320
In Eden came its malady,
By Adam's use its goodness died.
Through grim death goes each man, if he
Will cross here, as the Lord decide.'

I said, 'If you decide, my sweet,   325
On further grief, my life will fail.
What's lost, I find; what's gone, I greet;
To lose it now were mortal ail.
Must I let it go? What's this, to meet
And miss my pearl? O what avail   330
Is treasure, if its loss complete
Will later make men weep and wail?
I care not now is life is stale,
Nor if I'm exiled far and wide . . .
That there is great grief in my tale,   335
My pearl gone – who will not decide?'

'All you decide on is despair,'
Then said that girl. 'And why do so?
For when high sorrow fills the air,
A finer thing one may forgo.   340
Better to cross yourself in prayer,
And praise the Lord in bliss or woe.
Blind grief won't benefit you a hair;
Endure what you must undergo.
For though you fret as any doe,   345
And vent your agonies with wild stride,
Sometime you'll cease the to-and-fro:
And then accept what he decide.

'Decide against him and arraign,
His will won't alter in the least.   350
Not a hint of help you'll gain,
Though your sorrows never ceased.
Stop chafing then, no more complain.
His pity still may be released
By your sharp prayer. You may obtain   355
His mercy – and your pain be eased.
Pray very soon: he may be pleased
To turn your troubles fast aside.
For griefs to cool, or be increased,
All lies in him. He will decide.'   360

VII

To her decided words I gave
This answer: 'Let it not offend
My Lord, to hear me rant and rave.
My heart its sorrow of loss would spend
As springs let up a steady wave.   365
But in his mercy is my end.
Withhold your cold rebuke and grave,
Although my way I must amend,
My darling – and your comfort lend,
And in your pity think of this: 370
By you was I made sorrow's friend,
Though you were ground of all my bliss.

'My bliss, my anguish – you were these;
And much the greater was my moan.
When you were freed from all unease,   375
I never knew where my pearl had gone.
But now I see it, all griefs ease.
And since at parting we were at one,
No anger now – so may God please.
We meet so rarely by tree or stone.   380
You speak in a most courteous tone;
Mere dust am I, and much amiss.
But Christ's mercy, and Mary and John,
They are the ground of all my bliss.

'In bliss I see you blithely stand,   385
And I a man dejected, quite
Cast down. You little understand,
It seems, how painful is my plight.
But I am here now and at hand.
And so I ask you now outright,   390
What life is it, that in this land
You lead from morning until night?
For I am gladdened at the height
At which your station surely is.
It is the high road of delight   395
For me, and ground of all my bliss.'

'Now bliss be yours, sir,' then said she
Who was so lovely of limb and face,
'And you are welcome here to be
And walk; for now your words have grace.   400
But arrogance and vanity,
I vow, are unloved in this place:
My Lord hates wranglers. Those that he
Keeps near are meek in every case.
True meekness, then, will you embrace,   405
Going in the dwelling that is his.
My Lord the Lamb loves well its trace,
And he is ground of all my bliss.

'I lead a blissful life, you say;
You wonder, then, at what degree.   410
Now when your pearl fell down away
I was in tender infancy –
You know it well. In godly way
My Lord the Lamb then married me,
Crowned me queen in bliss to stay,   415
And so to all eternity.
His wife has all his property;
I am his in all and nothing miss.
His dear worth and high family
Are root and ground of all my bliss.'   420

VIII

'Blissful one – ' said I to her,
'Begging your pardon – is this true?
Are you the one who shall incur
Such honour – queen of heaven's blue?
To Mary of grace our prayers refer,   425
The maiden pure and mother too.
In some way her superior
There's none, to whom the crown falls due.
A sweetness all unique she knew;
"Arabia's Phoenix" then is she,   430
That flawless from its maker flew –
And so the Queen of courtesy.'

'Courteous queen,' that lovely one
Declared, and knelt, with face upturned;
'Who are past all comparison   435
Mother and maid – from whom is learned
Each grace!' She paused, and thereupon
Stood up; to me her speech returned.
'Sir, many here have sought and won
A prize, yet no-one is concerned   440
Her crowning reign be overturned:
Heaven, earth and hell are hers, all three.
Yet no-one's heritage has she spurned,
For she is Queen of courtesy.

'The court of the kingdom of God alive   445
Has a quality quite unknown
Outside itself. Who may arrive
Within its kingdom has its throne;
Yet no-one else shall they deprive,
But take joy in what others own,   450
And wish their crowns were each worth five
(If such improvement could be shown).
But she from whom was born and grown
Jesu – in the highest degree
She rules – yet no-one is cast down,   455
For she is Queen of courtesy.

'It is by courtesy, as said
Saint Paul, that we are all a part
Of Christ. As arm, leg, navel, head
Are body's own with binding art,   460
Just so a Christian soul is wed
To him who knows all secrets' heart.
Now what ill-feeling could be bred
Among your limbs – what feuds could start?
The head no mean looks will impart   465
Though ring on arm or finger be.
And we all love, not set apart,
King and Queen by courtesy.'

'Who'd doubt that courtesy is of
You all?' said I. 'And with it stays   470
Charity, true fellow-love.
Yet I repeat now that you raise
Yourself too high in heaven above:
A queen now, from such early days!
(Forgive me that my words reprove.)   475
What more, for one who bends his ways
Life-long, on bliss – and body flays,
To penance sworn unswervingly?
What richer honour him repays
Than being crowned king by courtesy?   480

IX

'That courtesy's too free of hand
You tell of – but your words mislead.
You lived not two years in our land,
And you could not recite the Creed
Or Paternoster understand;   485
Not pray, nor please God. Such misdeed –
A first-day queen! – for sure is banned:
The contrary I'll not concede.
Now miss, a countess' life to lead
Were fine, on high, this I'll affirm;   490
Or else a humbler life, indeed.
But a queen! It is too grand a term.'

'There's no term set to what he gives,'
That noble one then said to me.
'In all he does true rightness lives,   495
And justice tells in each decree.
Now Matthew fittingly conceives
The sense here, metaphorically;
And in your mass his words he leaves,
God's gospel true, for all to see.   500
"My kingdom in heaven is like," says he,
"A lord and his vineyard. Ripe the germ
For labour on the vineyard tree,
The year being at its aptest term.

"This vital term the labourers knew.   505
At earliest light the lord arose
And sought them out, and hired a crew
To work among his vineyard rows.
The pay, approved by common view,
A penny a day. Away go those   510
And toil and drudge with much ado,
Slicing, securing, strapping in close.
Three hours pass: then to market goes
The lord. Quite idle, as though infirm,
Men stand there. 'What, do you still doze?   515
And has the day no end or term?'

'Before the term of day we came,
And we have stood here since the sun
Arose' – they answered all the same,
'And we are given work by none.'   520
With them the lord began to frame
A contract. 'Go, and work each one
Among my vines; and past all blame
I'll pay at night what's fairly won.'
The lord had more work to be done,   525
Which by new men (still with a firm
Agreement) all day was begun;
Till day had nearly gone full term.

"At the known term of evensong,
The lord saw (when there was of light   530
One hour left) idle men, though strong:
He asked them simply and outright,
'Why are you idle all day long?'
No-one had bought their labour's right,
They told him. 'Young men, go along,   535
And in my vineyard use your might.'
Soon came dusk, to darken sight.
He said the wages he'd confirm.
The sun was down: it drew to night:
The day had ended, passed its term.   540

X

"To day's term and its end alert,
The lord said, 'Pay the company
Their due, good steward. And to avert
Grievance or complaint from any,
Line them up – let their desert   545
Be overall alike one penny.
Start with the latest to exert
Their labour – till all have their fee.'
But then the first put in a plea
That their day's work had taxed them sore,   550
'While these, an hour ago, were free!
It seems to us we should have more.

'For more is owed to us, we know,
Who have endured the noonday heat;
And you have set these in our row,   555
As us – with not two hours complete!'
To one the lord made answer though.
'My friend, you have a full receipt;
Take what is your own, and go.
A penny is promised to all. I repeat –   560
How are you damaged? by what deceit?
Did not the terms that sum ensure?
To stretch the terms do not entreat:
Then why should you now ask more?

'Moreover, one may use one's gift   565
As pleases one – so it's believed;
Or will your eye to evil shift
Because I'm true and have deceived
No-one?' 'Thus', said Christ, 'I'll sift
It out: the last are not bereaved,   570
But will be first; first last, though swift;
For many are called, but few received.' "
And thus they always have retrieved
A share, the men both late and poor;
And though their lives have little achieved,   575
The mercy of God is much the more.

'More joy and bliss have I herein,
Of life's full queenliness assured,
Than all the folk in the world could win
Who sought their justified reward.   580
Virtually now did I begin –
I came at evening to the yard –
And yet at once my whole pay in
I took, first thought of by my Lord.
But others there, who were ignored,   585
Had laboured long and hard before,
Yet still are waiting their award –
Perhaps to wait for long years more.'

Then I said more and spoke my mind.
'I find your words unreasonable.   590
If God's crown justice fall behind –
Holy Writ's no more than fable.
In the Psalter it is defined
In clear words unassailable:
"For each his true desert you find,   595
Almighty king most venerable."
If to pay you were preferable,
Who had not the long day to endure,
Then the less work, the more payable –
And so it goes on, the less, the more.'   600

XI

'Of more and less there's no debate
In God's rich kingdom,' she replied;
'Though man's reward be small or great,
The same is paid on every side.
The Lord's largesse will not abate;   605
Both harsh and sweet it is supplied:
It is ditch-water in full spate,
Or chasm-streams that never dried.
His liberal gift he will not hide
(Who rescues sinners from the trough)   610
From servants true. Their joy is wide –
For the grace of God is grace enough.

'To my discredit enough you've said:
I have taken my penny wrongly here;
I arrived too late; I deserve instead   615
A different station – a lower, I fear.
Tell me, when was a life ever led
(Though in prayer it were pure and clear)
Whose prize was not once forfeited
Of heaven bright – some way, somewhere?   620
And always more often, the older they were,
They left the clear path, trod the rough . . .
Mercy and grace must sometime steer,
For the grace of God is grace enough.

'Enough of grace have the innocent.   625
When born, to be baptised they go
To the water in turn. From this descent
The vineyard ground they come to know.
The day (to which there's darkness lent)
May soon to death's night dip. And so   630
Who did no wrong before they went –
Yet being his servants, were below –
The Lord full wages will bestow
On these. For why should he rebuff
Their effort? Nor will he be slow,   635
For the grace of God is grace enough.

'It's well enough known and understood
That man for bliss was first made fit;
But Adam forfeited that good
Because of an apple that he bit.   640
Then over men the sentence stood
Of grievous death. No benefit
Of joy was at their going; nor could
There be, from hell's fierce heat, respite.
Then came the cure and opposite.   645
For on the cross so sharp and tough
Rich blood ran – wonderful water with it –
The grace of God grew great enough.

'Enough there sprang up from that well,
Blood and water from the wide wound.   650
The blood bought off that furious hell,
And saved us from the death beyond.
The water is baptism, truth to tell,
That followed the lance so cruelly ground;
Those grave sins whereby Adam fell,   655
And all of us in death were drowned,
It washes away. In the whole world round
All promise of bliss was at first cut off:
But at a glad time again it is found;
And the grace of God is great enough.   660

XII

'Grace enough that man may have
Whose sins recur – if he repent:
But he must most contritely crave
Such end; and know grief's punishment.
But reason of right that cannot rave   665
Will always save the innocent.
A harsh decree God never gave
To guiltless ones. In the event
Of guilt, true sorrow must be spent,
If mercy of grace at last alight.   670
But he who knew not sin's descent,
The innocent one, is safe and right.

'To reason rightly in this case:
Two sorts are saved by God's good will.
The righteous one shall see his face;   675
The person who has done no ill
Will be there too. As in one place
The Psalter: "Lord, thy most high hill
What man may climb; or who embrace
Thy holy resting-place? He will,"   680
It says, "with hands that no harm spill;
A heart that, knowing no blame, is light.
Right there shall his step cease, be still."
The innocent one is safe by right.

'The righteous one will make his way   685
(It's certain) to the castle fair.
He does not waste his life away,
Nor dupes a neighbour with dark care.
And Solomon had this to say
Of him: that wisdom gains its share   690
Of honour. Thus he will not stray,
And so will glimpse God's heaven-in-air,
And know that lovely dwelling there
Is his – if hardiness have might.
But there's no doubt or danger where   695
The innocent one is safe by right.

'About the righteous, too, observes
David in Psalms (as you may see),
"Lord, judge never him who serves,
For none is justified to thee."   700
And so, at that court which reserves
All causes which may ever be
For trial – to plead the "right" deserves
Strong refutation . . . seeing that he
Who on the cross died bloodily,   705
Hands torn, enduring savage slight –
Will at your own trial set you free
For innocence and not by "right".

'Let him who reads aright, be told
(Since from a book can truth be taught)   710
How Jesus walked in days of old,
And men their children to him brought.
That he would touch them, nor withhold
His grace, they begged him and besought;
Disciples, hearing this, would scold,   715
Argue them off, and many thwart.
But Jesus gently cut them short:
'Enough, leave children in my sight;
The heavens are certain for their sort.'
The innocent ones are safe by right.   720

XIII

'Jesus called his followers in
(Who were by their own words beguiled),
And said his kingdom none could win
Unless he came there like a child.
No spot or stain of sullying sin,   725
Harmless, whole and undefiled,
For him will men at once unpin
The gate, upon his knocking mild.
There is the joy, by time untrialled,
The jeweller sought through stones of state;   730
Sold linen and wool and all goods piled
To buy him a pearl immaculate.

'This matchless pearl, that costs so dear
(The jeweller gave his every good),
Is like bright heaven's kingdom clear: 735
So said the Father of field and flood.
For it is spotless, pure, and sheer
In roundness, bright, serene of mood;
And to the righteous it's held near.
And look, here in my breast it's stood.   740
My Lord the Lamb, that shed his blood,
As peace's emblem there it set.
O give the mad world up for good,
Purchase your pearl immaculate.'

'Immaculate pearl, in pearls appearing,   745
Who made your form so fair?' said I.
'O you, the pearl of great price bearing,
Your beauty came not naturally.
Who made the clothes that you are wearing?
Pygmalion's art your looks defy;   750
And Aristotle's wit's despairing
To list your special quality.
Your colour passes the fleur-de-lys;
Your lovely gracious angel-state.
What kind of service, dear, tell me,   755
Performs a pearl immaculate?'

'My matchless Lamb, my destiny dear,
Improver of all' – so she pursued
Her speech – 'wed me; although, I fear,
That marriage would have once seemed crude.   760
But when I left your world so drear,
He called me to his beatitude:
'Sweetheart and loved one, come here;
No speck or taint in you is viewed.'
With power and beauty then imbued,   765
A pure one (in his blood that was let
He washed my clothes), I was endued
With the crown, and pearls immaculate.'

'O radiant immaculate bride,
Rich royal favours set among,   770
What is this Lamb, who would decide
To let you as his wife belong?
To stay exalted at his side
You've climbed so high, above a throng
Of fair-beneath-the-comb, who've tried   775
To live for Christ; and suffered long.
You down them all (and it seems wrong)
By marrying so – to dominate
All on your own, so bold and strong –
O matchless maid immaculate.'   780

XIV

' "Immaculate," ' then said to me
That lovely queen, 'I will allow,
And own quite unashamedly;
But "matchless queen" I disavow.
Wives to the Lamb in bliss are we –   785
A hundred and forty-four thousand now –
As in the Apocalypse you'll see;
Saint John saw them all, I vow.
His spirit dreamt and knew not how.
In wedding-dress then saw he them   790
On Sion's fair spur, on that hill-brow,
The new city of Jerusalem.

'Of Jerusalem I will tell.
If you would seek to know what sort
He is, my Lamb, my Lord, my jewel,   795
My bliss, my sweetheart – I exhort
You, read Isaiah. The prophet well
And movingly his meekness caught:
"That glorious innocent who fell
To murderous hands (no charge in court   800
Could hold) was to the slaughter brought
As though a sheep; and like a lamb
That's shorn, gripped fast – complaining nought
When the Jews judged in Jerusalem."

'In Jerusalem was he slain,   805
My lover, and bold villains tore
Him on the cross; and all our pain
And sorrow willingly he bore,
Our sad griefs taking up again.
His face, so fair, was buffeted sore.   810
For sin he set his life at vain,
Though he had none. To stoop him, score
His body, he allowed them – more,
To stretch him on a cumbrous beam;
And no complaint made, but forbore,   815
And died for us in Jerusalem.

'In Jerusalem, Jordan and Galilee
Did one baptise, the good Saint John,
And with Isaiah his words agree.
When Jesus up to him had gone,   820
He made for him this prophecy:
"Lo, God's Lamb, sure-set as stone,
The grave sins causing not to be
That all this world has carried on;
Who has himself committed none   825
And yet the whole of them will claim –
His birth, now, who can speak upon,
Our martyr in Jerusalem?"

'In Jerusalem taken for
A lamb was he (so two do say,   830
Isaiah and John, in witness sure),
My dear love, for his gentle way.
The third time now is one of awe.
(Apocalypse has on display
The words of witness.) Saint John saw   835
Him on the throne, where elders stay,
Opening the square-leaved book where it lay
Though sealed with seven seals at the hem.
And that sight must hold all in sway
In Hell, in Earth, and Jerusalem.   840

XV

'Jerusalem's Lamb had never stain
Of hue apart from whiteness bright;
No spot or speck could ever have lain
On that rich wool's abundant white.
And so a soul as wife may reign   845
That is of blemish free and light,
And though each day bring more in train,
We vie not, nor regret our plight;
But wish each one were five – it's right,
The more the merrier, I confess!   850
Our love in numbers large has might
To honour him more and never less.

'Less of bliss we none could bring
Who wear the pearl upon our breast;
Nor could one think of quarrelling   855
Who has the pearl-crown, spotless crest.
Our corpses are earth-mouldering –
Your grief cries out and cannot rest –
Yet we see clear in everything:
By one death all our hope was blessed.   860
The Lamb's our joy, there's no unrest,
And each mass heralds happiness.
Each one's bliss is glorious-best;
No-one's honour ever the less.

'And if you give less credit here   865
Than my account deserves, look where
John's words in Apocalypse appear.
"I saw him stand most noble and fair,
The Lamb on Sion, with maidens near,
A hundred and forty-four thousand, I swear.   870
On every forehead was written clear
The Lamb's name and his Father's there.
And a shout from the sky made me beware –
A voice like the racing of torrents in stress,
Or thunder that dark hills roll on air –   875
That sound, I believe, was nothing less.

"Nevertheless, though thunderously
It sounded, that voice sharp and strong,
They then began a melody.
The notes were near of that new song,   880
That excellent rich harmony,
As harp-notes harped from harp-strings long;
And hearing it was heavenly.
Most beautifully then in throng
Before God's throne, set right along   885
Beside the elders' seriousness,
And where the four meek beasts belong,
Such strains they sang, and never less.

"Nevertheless indeed there's none,
For all the knowledge that he knew,   890
Who might that song have once begun,
But only the Lamb's retinue.
Far from Earth redeemed and won
Are they, as God's first-fruits fall due,
To join the gentle noble one,   895
The Lamb, like him in speech and hue.
No lie they told, no tale untrue.
Now nothing can compel or press
That band to leave him, spotless too,
Their Lord – no instance, great or less." '   900

'My thanks are no whit less,' said I,
'My pearl – though I such questions pose.
Your wit supreme I should not try,
Whom Christ for bridal chamber chose.
Mere filth I am, as dust I lie,   905
And you so fair and fresh a rose,
And with this glorious bank nearby
From which life's freshness never goes.
Whom clear and simple ways enclose –
O let me ask a thing express.   910
In me a rough crossed nature shows.
Grant my prayer now nevertheless.

XVI

'Nevertheless I make clear call
On you, if you can see it done:
Since on your splendour lies no pall,   915
Do not deny my orison.
Is there no mansion, castle-wall,
Where you may meet and dwell, each one?
The royal Jerusalem you recall,
And David there was set upon   920
His throne: but by these woods there's none
Of Judaea's city, grand and great.
For one so spotless under the sun
What dwelling then, unstained in state?

'In speech you state a spotless throng   925
That crowds in thousands all about.
Does no city then belong
To that medley – such a rout?
From this indeed it were most wrong
A troop of bright jewels stay without;   930
But by these banks I linger along,
I see no dwelling hereabout.
You visit here, I cannot doubt,
To see this splendid stream in spate.
If there are buildings – lead me out   935
To that walled city, fair estate.'

'That estate in Judaea's land,'
This special person said to me,
'Is the city the Lamb planned
To suffer in most grievously –   940
Old Jerusalem, you understand –
For there the first sin ceased to be.
But the city set down by God's hand,
Jerusalem new, is that which he
In the Apocalypse lets us see.   945
The Lamb, all pure, has us to wait
Him there – a shining company
In his estate of spotless state.

'To state it plain and not concealed
By the same name for each of these   950
Two towns (to you known and revealed
As "city of God" or "vision of peace"),
In one of them our peace was sealed;
The Lamb chose it for his demise.
In the other peace is the only yield –   955
It lasts for ever and will not cease.
There, after our bodies' decease,
We press towards and congregate,
Where joy and honour will ever increase
For a retinue unstained in state.'   960

'Lady of state so tender and true,'
To that fair flower then I replied,
'Take me to it: that I may view
The blissful home where you abide.'
She said then, 'God forbids you to.   965
His tower you may not go inside;
But from the Lamb I have gained for you
(To his great favour I applied)
Leave to behold it from the outside.
Yet take not one step through the gate.   970
To walk in the street is quite denied
To one not pure, unstained in state.

XVII

'If this estate you'd see, therefore,
To this stream's source make your ascent;
And I shall follow from this shore,   975
Until a hill-top's imminent.'
I could not stay a moment more,
But under bright-leaved branches went
Up to the hill's brow, where I saw
The city, gazed on it intent.   980
Across the brook all brilliant
It lay, and brighter than sunbeams shone.
In the Apocalypse evident
It is, as tells the apostle John.

As John the Apostle it espied   985
I saw that city of wondrous name,
Jerusalem, new, rich, glorified,
As if from Heaven down it came.
All gleaming gold on every side,
Like polished glass it seemed aflame,   990
With splendid gems on the under-side.
Twelve layers lay there in the base-frame,
All finely joined, yet not the same;
Each tier was of a separate stone.
This same town has a rich acclaim   995
In Apocalypse from the apostle John.

By John's own list, in scripture's lore,
I knew the name in every case:
Jasper the first jewel I saw
That glowed green on the lowest base,   1000
The under-step, that all else bore.
Sapphire held the second space;
In the third tier, without flaw
Was chalcedony's clear pale grace;
Emerald's green in the fourth place;   1005
Fifth sardonyx then lay upon;
Sixth ruby – so we see him trace
In Apocalypse, the apostle John.

John adds to these the chrysolite
To be the base-frame's seventh stone;   1010
The eighth is beryl clear and white;
Ninth topaz of twin-coloured tone;
Set tenth is chrysoprase; the light
Of jacinth is eleventh shown;
The twelfth, that in dark days shines bright,   1015
The indigo and purple zone
Of amethyst, last under-stone.
Of jasper are the walls thereon
Like shining glass, as is made known
In Apocalypse by the apostle John.   1020

As John has told I saw it there:
The broad steep steps were twelve in all;
The city stood above, full square,
Exactly as long as broad as tall.
Gold streets, that yet were sheer and bare   1025
As glass; around, the jasper wall
Had shine of glair. Rich jewels made fair
The walls within beyond recall.
The full square of this heavenly hall,
Height, length and breadth reached, all at one,   1030
Twelve thousand furlongs overall,
Its measure seen by the apostle John.

XVIII

As John leaves word so I saw more.
Along each side there stood three gates;
So twelve in total there I saw;   1035
And decked with splendid metal plates
The portals were. Of pearl past flaw,
With a brightness that never abates,
Was each gate made; and each, too, bore
A name. Inscription there creates   1040
Israel's children, by birth-dates
Set down: the eldest is first shown.
Such light the streets illuminates
That they need neither sun nor moon.

Not sun nor moon had cause to be;   1045
God himself was their lamp-light,
The Lamb their lantern, certainly;
Through him the town shone brilliant-bright.
Through wall and dwelling I could see,
All transparent; nothing stopped the light.   1050
The high throne, festooned gloriously,
Was clear to view and lay in sight
(As John the apostle did plainly write);
And God's high figure sat thereon.
From the throne a river ran outright,   1055
Brighter than both the sun and moon.

Never shone sun and moon so fair
As that full flood from that ground shone;
Swiftly it rushed down everywhere,
With not a speck of dirt upon.   1060
No church stood there anywhere,
No temple, chapel-place – not one;
The Almighty was their minster there,
The Lamb the sacrifice undergone
To be refreshment. Opening on   1065
The roadways, gates were ever wide thrown . . .
But to this refuge enters none
With any spot beneath the moon.

From there the moon derives no light;
Too pitted she is, too ugly and drear;   1070
And also there is never night.
Why should the moon her circuit steer
With that power to compete, to fight,
That on the stream-top dazzles sheer?
The planets are in too poor a plight,   1075
The sun is much too dim, unclear.
About the stream trees brilliant-clear
Stand out; and life's twelve fruits they soon
Bring forth. They bear twelve times a year,
Renewing themselves at each month's moon.   1080

Beneath the moon the immensity
Of awe, a body would fordo –
As when I looked upon that city,
Its marvellous fashioned state, I knew.
As dazed quail stood I quietly   1085
In wonder at that noble view.
Not turmoil, nor tranquillity
I felt, so was I flooded through
With radiant light. Now this is true:
Had a bodily form met with that boon,   1090
Though skilled men did all they might do,
His life were lost beneath the moon.

XIX

Just as the mighty moon will rise
Before the daylight's down away,
So suddenly before my eyes   1095
A procession was on its way.
No hint had I had or surmise.
This noble city of rich array
Was full of maidens in the same guise
As my crowned lovely one's display;   1100
And all were crowned in the same way,
White clothes and pearls they wore, set right.
On each one's breast firm-fastened lay
The lovely pearl with great delight.

With great delight they went along 1105
On golden streets that gleamed as glass,
A hundred thousand in the throng;
And matching all their raiment was.
To note one happiest look, were wrong.
The Lamb their leader in first place 1110
With clothing like rich pearl was hung;
Seven horns of bright red gold he has.
Towards the throne I saw them pass;
Such crowds were no unseemly sight;
But gentle as maidens are at mass, 1115
So they surged on with great delight.

Delight they in his progress found
Were far too great for me to tell.
As he approached, down on the ground
About his feet, the elders fell; 1120
Legions of angels summoned round
Scattered incense of sweet smell;
Then worship and joy took a new sound;
All sang to praise that shining jewel.
The sound could strike through the Earth to Hell 1125
As the Virtue-Angels their joy recite.
That I should praise the Lamb as well,
In truth I took a great delight.

Delight to see him entered me,
And much amazement there beside.   1130
The finest, the gentlest and noblest was he,
More than the power of words can provide.
His clothes clear white, so graciously
He bore himself, so far from pride.
But a wound all wide and wet to see   1135
Was at his heart, through the ripped hide.
His blood burst out from the white side.
Alas, who did that deed of spite?
Any man's breast would have burnt up, died
Before in that he took delight.   1140

The Lamb's delight no-one would care
To doubt, as he was not dismayed,
But of his wound seemed unaware,
In highest happiness arrayed.
I looked about his company fair,   1145
The sheer life that their lives displayed;
Then I my little queen saw there,
Who I thought by me in the valley had stayed.
Lord, much the merriment she made
Among her friends, who was so white!   1150
That sight made me resolve to wade
For a longing of love, in great delight.

XX

Delight assailed me, eye and ear,
My human mind to madness slid;
Across the stream when I saw my dear   1155
I must be there. What could forbid
My plunging in in swift career
To swim the rest? No blow undid
The plan, I thought – brought me up sheer:
And so – though it my life fordid –   1160
I must rush in. Yet as I did,
That headlong action brought displeasure,
And of my purpose was I rid.
It was not to my Prince's pleasure.

It pleased him not that I forsook   1165
My wits, and at the stream had sped.
That wild charge though I undertook,
I was from it abruptly led.
For just as I dashed up to the brook,
My dream was by that suddenness shed.   1170
Then woke I in that grassy nook;
Upon the hillock rested my head
Where my pearl in the ground was fled.
I reached out, caught in grief's fierce seizure;
Then sighing, to myself I said,   1175
'Now all be to that Prince's pleasure.'

It pleased me not at all to be
Shut out from that fair citadel;
So rich and so alive to see
Was all that in my dream befell.   1180
A heavy longing conquered me,
And I cried out from sorrow's cell,
'O pearl of noble royalty,
So did your lovely words excel
In vision true! If as you tell,   1185
You are set so in garland's treasure –
Though I am cast down – it were well
That you are to that Prince's pleasure.'

That Prince's pleasure had I observed,
A greater licence had I not yearned,   1190
But had held true and never swerved,
As that fair pearl was so concerned,
Perhaps – from God's presence not reserved –
More of his mysteries I had learned.
But man seeks more than is deserved;   1195
And so my joy was overturned,
And from those regions was I spurned
That last eternity's length and leisure.
Lord, all who have against you turned
Are mad, or who oppose your pleasure.   1200

To please the Prince, allay his mind,
Good Christians do it easily.
A God, a Lord, a friend most kind,
I know that day and night is he.
And so this fortune did I find   1205
Upon the hill where sorrowfully
I lay. My pearl then I consigned
To God, blessed both by Christ and me.
Him does our priest bear visibly
As bread and wine in daily measure,   1210
Who bids us his good labourers be,
And precious pearls fit for his pleasure.

AMEN.   AMEN.